E
921
Was
C1

$20.00

Mara, Wil
George Washington

REINBERG SCHOOL LIBRARY
3425 N. MAJOR AVENUE
CHICAGO, IL 60634

35600000064952

DEMCO

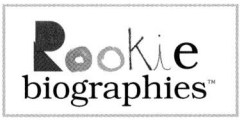

George Washington

By Wil Mara

Consultants
Nanci R. Vargus, Ed.D.
Primary Multiage Teacher
Decatur Township Schools, Indianapolis, Indiana

Katharine A. Kane, Reading Specialist
Former Language Arts Coordinator
San Diego County Office of Education

Children's Press®
A Division of Scholastic Inc.
New York Toronto London Auckland Sydney
Mexico City New Delhi Hong Kong
Danbury, Connecticut

Designer: Herman Adler Design
Photo Researcher: Caroline Anderson
The photo on the cover shows George Washington.

Library of Congress Cataloging-in-Publication Data

Mara, Wil.
George Washington / by Wil Mara.
p. cm. — (Rookie biographies)
Includes index.
Summary: An introduction to the life of George Washington, who became the first president of the United States after leading the American military in the Revolutionary War against England.
ISBN 0-516-22519-7 (lib. bdg.) 0-516-27335-3 (pbk.)
1. Washington, George, 1732-1799—Juvenile literature. 2. Presidents—United States—Biography—Juvenile literature. [1. Washington, George, 1732-1799. 2. Presidents.] I. Title. II. Series
E312.66 .M27 2002
973.4'1'092—dc21

2001008318

©2002 Children's Press
A Division of Scholastic Inc.
All rights reserved. Published simultaneously in Canada.
Printed in the United States of America.

CHILDREN'S PRESS, AND ROOKIE BIOGRAPHIES™, and associated logos are trademarks and or registered trademarks of Grolier Publishing Co., Inc. SCHOLASTIC and associated logos are trademarks and or registered trademarks of Scholastic Inc.

1 2 3 4 5 6 7 8 9 10 R 11 10 09 08 07 06 05 04 03 02

George Washington was
our first president.

He was born in Virginia on February 22, 1732.

Back then, America was ruled by England. Virginia was a colony, not a state. The people who lived in America were called colonists.

Washington's family owned a big farm. Young George enjoyed farm work.

He also liked to study. His favorite subject was math.

REINBERG SCHOOL LIBRARY
3425 N. MAJOR AVENUE
CHICAGO, IL 60634

George Washington joined the military, or armed forces, when he was twenty years old. His first job was to deliver a note to a man more than three hundred miles away!

Washington left the military in 1759. Then he married Martha Custis.

He became a politician (pol-uh-TISH-uhn). A politician is elected, or chosen, to work for the government.

At this time, the English government began to tax the tea and stamps it sold to the American colonies. This made the colonists angry. They wanted to be free from England's laws.

A war began between England and the American colonies. It was called the Revolutionary (rev-uh-LOO-shuhn-air-ee) War. Washington was asked to lead the military during this war.

Washington was a good leader. The colonies won the war in 1783. America became a free country.

George Washington was a hero.

In 1789, he was elected to be America's first president.

It was hard to be president of a new country. The government was very small.

Washington found smart and honest people to work with him.

Copyright, 1876, by Currier & Ives, N.Y.
GEORGE WASHINGTON.
GENL HENRY KNOX, Secy of War
ALEXANDER HAMILTON, Secy of the Treasury
THOMAS JEFFERSON, Secy of State.
EDMUND RANDOLPH, Attorney General.
WASHINGTON AND HIS CABINET.

CONTINENTAL DOLLAR

1776

America also needed its own money. There were no American coins or paper bills. Washington passed a law that let the government make some.

Washington worked as president for four years. Then he wanted to go back to Virginia. But many people asked Washington to stay for four more years. He did.

Washington went back to Virginia to be with his family in 1797. He died there on December 14, 1799.

Today, we think of George Washington as "The Father of Our Country."

America's capital city, Washington, D.C., is named after him.

Words You Know

coins

colonists

hero

military

president

Washington, D.C.

George Washington

Index

America, 5, 13, 14, 17, 23
capital cities, 28
coins, 22, 23
colonies, 5, 13, 14, 17
colonists, 5, 12, 13
Custis, Martha, 10, 11
death, 27
England, 5, 13, 14
farms, 6
"Father of Our Country," 28
government, 10, 20, 23
heroes, 18
marriage, 10, 11
math, 6
military, 8, 9, 10, 14, 15
money, 22, 23
politicians, 10
presidents, 3, 19, 20, 24
Revolutionary War, 14, 17
stamps, 13
study, 6
tax, 13
tea, 13
Virginia, 5, 24, 27
Washington, D.C., 28, 29

About the Author

Wil Mara has written over fifty books. He writes fiction and nonfiction for both children and adults. He lives with his wife and three daughters in northern New Jersey.

Photo Credits

Photographs © 2002: Art Resource, NY: cover; Bridgeman Art Library International Ltd., London/New York: 25, 31 left (Brooklyn Museum of Art, New York, USA), 11 (Private Collection); Hulton Archive/Getty Images: 18, 30 bottom left; North Wind Picture Archives: 8, 15, 26, 30 bottom right; Photo Researchers, NY/Library of Congress: 21; Photri Inc.: 16, 22, 29, 30 top left, 31 bottom left; Stock Montage, Inc.: 7, 12, 30 top right; Superstock, Inc.: 3 (New Bedford Public Library), 4 (Philadelphia Free Library/A.K.G. Berlin), 19, 31 top left.

REINBERG SCHOOL LIBRARY
3425 N. MAJOR AVENUE
CHICAGO, IL 60634